This Planner Belongs To:

Name:

Phone:

Address:

Email:

Emergency contact:

Name:

Phone:

Address:

Email:

Copyright ©2018
Ritchie Media
Peterborough, ON, Canada

2018

January
M	T	W	T	F	S	S
1	2	3	4	5	6	7
8	9	10	11	12	13	14
15	16	17	18	19	20	21
22	23	24	25	26	27	28
29	30	31				

February
M	T	W	T	F	S	S
			1	2	3	4
5	6	7	8	9	10	11
12	13	14	15	16	17	18
19	20	21	22	23	24	25
26	27	28				

March
M	T	W	T	F	S	S
			1	2	3	4
5	6	7	8	9	10	11
12	13	14	15	16	17	18
19	20	21	22	23	24	25
26	27	28	29	30	31	

April
M	T	W	T	F	S	S
						1
2	3	4	5	6	7	8
9	10	11	12	13	14	15
16	17	18	19	20	21	22
23	24	25	26	27	28	29
30						

May
M	T	W	T	F	S	S
	1	2	3	4	5	6
7	8	9	10	11	12	13
14	15	16	17	18	19	20
21	22	23	24	25	26	27
28	29	30	31			

June
M	T	W	T	F	S	S
				1	2	3
4	5	6	7	8	9	10
11	12	13	14	15	16	17
18	19	20	21	22	23	24
25	26	27	28	29	30	

July
M	T	W	T	F	S	S
						1
2	3	4	5	6	7	8
9	10	11	12	13	14	15
16	17	18	19	20	21	22
23	24	25	26	27	28	29
30	31					

August
M	T	W	T	F	S	S
		1	2	3	4	5
6	7	8	9	10	11	12
13	14	15	16	17	18	19
20	21	22	23	24	25	26
27	28	29	30	31		

September
M	T	W	T	F	S	S
					1	2
3	4	5	6	7	8	9
10	11	12	13	14	15	16
17	18	19	20	21	22	23
24	25	26	27	28	29	30

October
M	T	W	T	F	S	S
1	2	3	4	5	6	7
8	9	10	11	12	13	14
15	16	17	18	19	20	21
22	23	24	25	26	27	28
29	30	31				

November
M	T	W	T	F	S	S
			1	2	3	4
5	6	7	8	9	10	11
12	13	14	15	16	17	18
19	20	21	22	23	24	25
26	27	28	29	30		

December
M	T	W	T	F	S	S
					1	2
3	4	5	6	7	8	9
10	11	12	13	14	15	16
17	18	19	20	21	22	23
24	25	26	27	28	29	30
31						

2019

January
M	T	W	T	F	S	S
31	1	2	3	4	5	6
7	8	9	10	11	12	13
14	15	16	17	18	19	20
21	22	23	24	25	26	27
28	29	30	31	1	2	3
4	5	6	7	8	9	10

February
M	T	W	T	F	S	S
28	29	30	31	1	2	3
4	5	6	7	8	9	10
11	12	13	14	15	16	17
18	19	20	21	22	23	24
25	26	27	28	1	2	3
4	5	6	7	8	9	10

March
M	T	W	T	F	S	S
25	26	27	28	1	2	3
4	5	6	7	8	9	10
11	12	13	14	15	16	17
18	19	20	21	22	23	24
25	26	27	28	29	30	31
1	2	3	4	5	6	7

April
M	T	W	T	F	S	S
1	2	3	4	5	6	7
8	9	10	11	12	13	14
15	16	17	18	19	20	21
22	23	24	25	26	27	28
29	30	1	2	3	4	5
6	7	8	9	10	11	12

May
M	T	W	T	F	S	S
29	30	1	2	3	4	5
6	7	8	9	10	11	12
13	14	15	16	17	18	19
20	21	22	23	24	25	26
27	28	29	30	31	1	2
3	4	5	6	7	8	9

June
M	T	W	T	F	S	S
27	28	29	30	31	1	2
3	4	5	6	7	8	9
10	11	12	13	14	15	16
17	18	19	20	21	22	23
24	25	26	27	28	29	30
1	2	3	4	5	6	7

July
M	T	W	T	F	S	S
1	2	3	4	5	6	7
8	9	10	11	12	13	14
15	16	17	18	19	20	21
22	23	24	25	26	27	28
29	30	31	1	2	3	4
5	6	7	8	9	10	11

August
M	T	W	T	F	S	S
29	30	31	1	2	3	4
5	6	7	8	9	10	11
12	13	14	15	16	17	18
19	20	21	22	23	24	25
26	27	28	29	30	31	1
2	3	4	5	6	7	8

September
M	T	W	T	F	S	S
26	27	28	29	30	31	1
2	3	4	5	6	7	8
9	10	11	12	13	14	15
16	17	18	19	20	21	22
23	24	25	26	27	28	29
30	1	2	3	4	5	6

October
M	T	W	T	F	S	S
30	1	2	3	4	5	6
7	8	9	10	11	12	13
14	15	16	17	18	19	20
21	22	23	24	25	26	27
28	29	30	31	1	2	3
4	5	6	7	8	9	10

November
M	T	W	T	F	S	S
28	29	30	31	1	2	3
4	5	6	7	8	9	10
11	12	13	14	15	16	17
18	19	20	21	22	23	24
25	26	27	28	29	30	1
2	3	4	5	6	7	8

December
M	T	W	T	F	S	S
25	26	27	28	29	30	1
2	3	4	5	6	7	8
9	10	11	12	13	14	15
16	17	18	19	20	21	22
23	24	25	26	27	28	29
30	31	1	2	3	4	5

Important Contacts

Name:

Phone:

Address:

Email:

Name:

Phone:

Address:

Email:

Name:

Phone:

Address:

Email:

Name:

Phone:

Address:

Email:

Name:

Phone:

Address:

Email:

Notes

Week of: _____

Monday		Morning		Afternoon		Evening
	8:00		1:00		6:00	
	9:00		2:00		7:00	
	10:00		3:00		8:00	
	11:00		4:00		9:00	
	12:00		5:00		10:00	

Notes:

Priorities:

Tuesday		Morning		Afternoon		Evening
	8:00		1:00		6:00	
	9:00		2:00		7:00	
	10:00		3:00		8:00	
	11:00		4:00		9:00	
	12:00		5:00		10:00	

Notes:

Priorities:

Wednesday		Morning		Afternoon		Evening
	8:00		1:00		6:00	
	9:00		2:00		7:00	
	10:00		3:00		8:00	
	11:00		4:00		9:00	
	12:00		5:00		10:00	

Notes:

Priorities:

Thursday		Morning		Afternoon		Evening
	8:00		1:00		6:00	
	9:00		2:00		7:00	
	10:00		3:00		8:00	
	11:00		4:00		9:00	
	12:00		5:00		10:00	

Notes:

Priorities:

Friday		Morning		Afternoon		Evening
	8:00		1:00		6:00	
	9:00		2:00		7:00	
	10:00		3:00		8:00	
	11:00		4:00		9:00	
	12:00		5:00		10:00	

Notes:

Priorities:

Weekend		Morning		Afternoon		Evening
	8:00		1:00		6:00	
	9:00		2:00		7:00	
	10:00		3:00		8:00	
	11:00		4:00		9:00	
	12:00		5:00		10:00	

Notes:

Priorities:

Notes

Week of: _____

Monday		Morning		Afternoon		Evening
	8:00		1:00		6:00	
	9:00		2:00		7:00	
	10:00		3:00		8:00	
	11:00		4:00		9:00	
	12:00		5:00		10:00	

Notes:

Priorities:

Tuesday		Morning		Afternoon		Evening
	8:00		1:00		6:00	
	9:00		2:00		7:00	
	10:00		3:00		8:00	
	11:00		4:00		9:00	
	12:00		5:00		10:00	

Notes:

Priorities:

Wednesday		Morning		Afternoon		Evening
	8:00		1:00		6:00	
	9:00		2:00		7:00	
	10:00		3:00		8:00	
	11:00		4:00		9:00	
	12:00		5:00		10:00	

Notes:

Priorities:

Thursday		Morning		Afternoon		Evening
	8:00		1:00		6:00	
	9:00		2:00		7:00	
	10:00		3:00		8:00	
	11:00		4:00		9:00	
	12:00		5:00		10:00	

Notes:

Priorities:

Friday		Morning		Afternoon		Evening
	8:00		1:00		6:00	
	9:00		2:00		7:00	
	10:00		3:00		8:00	
	11:00		4:00		9:00	
	12:00		5:00		10:00	

Notes:

Priorities:

Weekend		Morning		Afternoon		Evening
	8:00		1:00		6:00	
	9:00		2:00		7:00	
	10:00		3:00		8:00	
	11:00		4:00		9:00	
	12:00		5:00		10:00	

Notes:

Priorities:

Notes

Week of: _____

Monday		Morning		Afternoon		Evening
	8:00		1:00		6:00	
	9:00		2:00		7:00	
	10:00		3:00		8:00	
	11:00		4:00		9:00	
	12:00		5:00		10:00	

Notes:

Priorities:

Tuesday		Morning		Afternoon		Evening
	8:00		1:00		6:00	
	9:00		2:00		7:00	
	10:00		3:00		8:00	
	11:00		4:00		9:00	
	12:00		5:00		10:00	

Notes:

Priorities:

Wednesday		Morning		Afternoon		Evening
	8:00		1:00		6:00	
	9:00		2:00		7:00	
	10:00		3:00		8:00	
	11:00		4:00		9:00	
	12:00		5:00		10:00	

Notes:

Priorities:

Thursday		Morning		Afternoon		Evening
	8:00		1:00		6:00	
	9:00		2:00		7:00	
	10:00		3:00		8:00	
	11:00		4:00		9:00	
	12:00		5:00		10:00	

Notes:

Priorities:

Friday		Morning		Afternoon		Evening
8:00		1:00		6:00		
9:00		2:00		7:00		
10:00		3:00		8:00		
11:00		4:00		9:00		
12:00		5:00		10:00		

Notes:

Priorities:

Weekend		Morning		Afternoon		Evening
8:00		1:00		6:00		
9:00		2:00		7:00		
10:00		3:00		8:00		
11:00		4:00		9:00		
12:00		5:00		10:00		

Notes:

Priorities:

Notes

Week of: _____

Monday		Morning		Afternoon		Evening
	8:00		1:00		6:00	
	9:00		2:00		7:00	
	10:00		3:00		8:00	
	11:00		4:00		9:00	
	12:00		5:00		10:00	

Notes:

Priorities:

Tuesday		Morning		Afternoon		Evening
	8:00		1:00		6:00	
	9:00		2:00		7:00	
	10:00		3:00		8:00	
	11:00		4:00		9:00	
	12:00		5:00		10:00	

Notes:

Priorities:

Wednesday		Morning		Afternoon		Evening
8:00		1:00		6:00		
9:00		2:00		7:00		
10:00		3:00		8:00		
11:00		4:00		9:00		
12:00		5:00		10:00		

Notes:

Priorities:

Thursday		Morning		Afternoon		Evening
8:00		1:00		6:00		
9:00		2:00		7:00		
10:00		3:00		8:00		
11:00		4:00		9:00		
12:00		5:00		10:00		

Notes:

Priorities:

Friday		Morning		Afternoon		Evening
	8:00		1:00		6:00	
	9:00		2:00		7:00	
	10:00		3:00		8:00	
	11:00		4:00		9:00	
	12:00		5:00		10:00	

Notes:

Priorities:

Weekend		Morning		Afternoon		Evening
	8:00		1:00		6:00	
	9:00		2:00		7:00	
	10:00		3:00		8:00	
	11:00		4:00		9:00	
	12:00		5:00		10:00	

Notes:

Priorities:

Notes

Week of: _____

Monday		Morning		Afternoon		Evening
	8:00		1:00		6:00	
	9:00		2:00		7:00	
	10:00		3:00		8:00	
	11:00		4:00		9:00	
	12:00		5:00		10:00	

Notes:

Priorities:

Tuesday		Morning		Afternoon		Evening
	8:00		1:00		6:00	
	9:00		2:00		7:00	
	10:00		3:00		8:00	
	11:00		4:00		9:00	
	12:00		5:00		10:00	

Notes:

Priorities:

Wednesday		Morning		Afternoon		Evening
	8:00		1:00		6:00	
	9:00		2:00		7:00	
	10:00		3:00		8:00	
	11:00		4:00		9:00	
	12:00		5:00		10:00	

Notes:

Priorities:

Thursday		Morning		Afternoon		Evening
	8:00		1:00		6:00	
	9:00		2:00		7:00	
	10:00		3:00		8:00	
	11:00		4:00		9:00	
	12:00		5:00		10:00	

Notes:

Priorities:

Friday		Morning		Afternoon		Evening
	8:00		1:00		6:00	
	9:00		2:00		7:00	
	10:00		3:00		8:00	
	11:00		4:00		9:00	
	12:00		5:00		10:00	

Notes:

Priorities:

Weekend		Morning		Afternoon		Evening
	8:00		1:00		6:00	
	9:00		2:00		7:00	
	10:00		3:00		8:00	
	11:00		4:00		9:00	
	12:00		5:00		10:00	

Notes:

Priorities:

Notes

Week of: _____

Monday		Morning		Afternoon		Evening
	8:00		1:00		6:00	
	9:00		2:00		7:00	
	10:00		3:00		8:00	
	11:00		4:00		9:00	
	12:00		5:00		10:00	

Notes:

Priorities:

Tuesday		Morning		Afternoon		Evening
	8:00		1:00		6:00	
	9:00		2:00		7:00	
	10:00		3:00		8:00	
	11:00		4:00		9:00	
	12:00		5:00		10:00	

Notes:

Priorities:

Wednesday		Morning		Afternoon		Evening	
	8:00		1:00		6:00		
	9:00		2:00		7:00		
	10:00		3:00		8:00		
	11:00		4:00		9:00		
	12:00		5:00		10:00		

Notes:

Priorities:

Thursday		Morning		Afternoon		Evening	
	8:00		1:00		6:00		
	9:00		2:00		7:00		
	10:00		3:00		8:00		
	11:00		4:00		9:00		
	12:00		5:00		10:00		

Notes:

Priorities:

Friday		Morning		Afternoon		Evening
	8:00		1:00		6:00	
	9:00		2:00		7:00	
	10:00		3:00		8:00	
	11:00		4:00		9:00	
	12:00		5:00		10:00	

Notes:

Priorities:

Weekend		Morning		Afternoon		Evening
	8:00		1:00		6:00	
	9:00		2:00		7:00	
	10:00		3:00		8:00	
	11:00		4:00		9:00	
	12:00		5:00		10:00	

Notes:

Priorities:

Notes

Week of: _____

Monday		Morning		Afternoon		Evening
	8:00		1:00		6:00	
	9:00		2:00		7:00	
	10:00		3:00		8:00	
	11:00		4:00		9:00	
	12:00		5:00		10:00	

Notes:

Priorities:

Tuesday		Morning		Afternoon		Evening
	8:00		1:00		6:00	
	9:00		2:00		7:00	
	10:00		3:00		8:00	
	11:00		4:00		9:00	
	12:00		5:00		10:00	

Notes:

Priorities:

Wednesday		Morning		Afternoon		Evening
	8:00		1:00		6:00	
	9:00		2:00		7:00	
	10:00		3:00		8:00	
	11:00		4:00		9:00	
	12:00		5:00		10:00	

Notes:

Priorities:

Thursday		Morning		Afternoon		Evening
	8:00		1:00		6:00	
	9:00		2:00		7:00	
	10:00		3:00		8:00	
	11:00		4:00		9:00	
	12:00		5:00		10:00	

Notes:

Priorities:

Friday		Morning		Afternoon		Evening
	8:00		1:00		6:00	
	9:00		2:00		7:00	
	10:00		3:00		8:00	
	11:00		4:00		9:00	
	12:00		5:00		10:00	

Notes:

Priorities:

Weekend		Morning		Afternoon		Evening
	8:00		1:00		6:00	
	9:00		2:00		7:00	
	10:00		3:00		8:00	
	11:00		4:00		9:00	
	12:00		5:00		10:00	

Notes:

Priorities:

Notes

Week of: _____

Monday		Morning		Afternoon		Evening
	8:00		1:00		6:00	
	9:00		2:00		7:00	
	10:00		3:00		8:00	
	11:00		4:00		9:00	
	12:00		5:00		10:00	

Notes:

Priorities:

Tuesday		Morning		Afternoon		Evening
	8:00		1:00		6:00	
	9:00		2:00		7:00	
	10:00		3:00		8:00	
	11:00		4:00		9:00	
	12:00		5:00		10:00	

Notes:

Priorities:

Wednesday		Morning		Afternoon		Evening	
	8:00		1:00		6:00		
	9:00		2:00		7:00		
	10:00		3:00		8:00		
	11:00		4:00		9:00		
	12:00		5:00		10:00		

Notes:

Priorities:

Thursday		Morning		Afternoon		Evening	
	8:00		1:00		6:00		
	9:00		2:00		7:00		
	10:00		3:00		8:00		
	11:00		4:00		9:00		
	12:00		5:00		10:00		

Notes:

Priorities:

Friday		Morning		Afternoon		Evening	
	8:00		1:00		6:00		
	9:00		2:00		7:00		
	10:00		3:00		8:00		
	11:00		4:00		9:00		
	12:00		5:00		10:00		

Notes:

Priorities:

Weekend		Morning		Afternoon		Evening	
	8:00		1:00		6:00		
	9:00		2:00		7:00		
	10:00		3:00		8:00		
	11:00		4:00		9:00		
	12:00		5:00		10:00		

Notes:

Priorities:

Notes

Week of: _____

Monday		Morning		Afternoon		Evening
	8:00		1:00		6:00	
	9:00		2:00		7:00	
	10:00		3:00		8:00	
	11:00		4:00		9:00	
	12:00		5:00		10:00	

Notes:

Priorities:

Tuesday		Morning		Afternoon		Evening
	8:00		1:00		6:00	
	9:00		2:00		7:00	
	10:00		3:00		8:00	
	11:00		4:00		9:00	
	12:00		5:00		10:00	

Notes:

Priorities:

Wednesday		Morning		Afternoon		Evening
	8:00		1:00		6:00	
	9:00		2:00		7:00	
	10:00		3:00		8:00	
	11:00		4:00		9:00	
	12:00		5:00		10:00	

Notes:

Priorities:

Thursday		Morning		Afternoon		Evening
	8:00		1:00		6:00	
	9:00		2:00		7:00	
	10:00		3:00		8:00	
	11:00		4:00		9:00	
	12:00		5:00		10:00	

Notes:

Priorities:

Friday		Morning		Afternoon		Evening
	8:00		1:00		6:00	
	9:00		2:00		7:00	
	10:00		3:00		8:00	
	11:00		4:00		9:00	
	12:00		5:00		10:00	

Notes:

Priorities:

Weekend		Morning		Afternoon		Evening
	8:00		1:00		6:00	
	9:00		2:00		7:00	
	10:00		3:00		8:00	
	11:00		4:00		9:00	
	12:00		5:00		10:00	

Notes:

Priorities:

Notes

Week of: _____

Monday		Morning		Afternoon		Evening	
	8:00		1:00		6:00	
	9:00		2:00		7:00	
	10:00		3:00		8:00	
	11:00		4:00		9:00	
	12:00		5:00		10:00	

Notes:

Priorities:

Tuesday		Morning		Afternoon		Evening	
	8:00		1:00		6:00	
	9:00		2:00		7:00	
	10:00		3:00		8:00	
	11:00		4:00		9:00	
	12:00		5:00		10:00	

Notes:

Priorities:

Wednesday		Morning		Afternoon		Evening
	8:00		1:00		6:00	
	9:00		2:00		7:00	
	10:00		3:00		8:00	
	11:00		4:00		9:00	
	12:00		5:00		10:00	

Notes:

Priorities:

Thursday		Morning		Afternoon		Evening
	8:00		1:00		6:00	
	9:00		2:00		7:00	
	10:00		3:00		8:00	
	11:00		4:00		9:00	
	12:00		5:00		10:00	

Notes:

Priorities:

Friday		Morning		Afternoon		Evening
	8:00		1:00		6:00	
	9:00		2:00		7:00	
	10:00		3:00		8:00	
	11:00		4:00		9:00	
	12:00		5:00		10:00	

Notes:

Priorities:

Weekend		Morning		Afternoon		Evening
	8:00		1:00		6:00	
	9:00		2:00		7:00	
	10:00		3:00		8:00	
	11:00		4:00		9:00	
	12:00		5:00		10:00	

Notes:

Priorities:

Notes

Week of: _____

Monday

	Morning		Afternoon		Evening
8:00		1:00		6:00	
9:00		2:00		7:00	
10:00		3:00		8:00	
11:00		4:00		9:00	
12:00		5:00		10:00	

Notes:

Priorities:

Tuesday

	Morning		Afternoon		Evening
8:00		1:00		6:00	
9:00		2:00		7:00	
10:00		3:00		8:00	
11:00		4:00		9:00	
12:00		5:00		10:00	

Notes:

Priorities:

Wednesday		Morning		Afternoon		Evening
	8:00		1:00		6:00	
	9:00		2:00		7:00	
	10:00		3:00		8:00	
	11:00		4:00		9:00	
	12:00		5:00		10:00	

Notes:

Priorities:

Thursday		Morning		Afternoon		Evening
	8:00		1:00		6:00	
	9:00		2:00		7:00	
	10:00		3:00		8:00	
	11:00		4:00		9:00	
	12:00		5:00		10:00	

Notes:

Priorities:

Friday		Morning		Afternoon		Evening
	8:00		1:00		6:00	
	9:00		2:00		7:00	
	10:00		3:00		8:00	
	11:00		4:00		9:00	
	12:00		5:00		10:00	

Notes:

Priorities:

Weekend		Morning		Afternoon		Evening
	8:00		1:00		6:00	
	9:00		2:00		7:00	
	10:00		3:00		8:00	
	11:00		4:00		9:00	
	12:00		5:00		10:00	

Notes:

Priorities:

Notes

Week of: _____

Monday		Morning		Afternoon		Evening
	8:00		1:00		6:00	
	9:00		2:00		7:00	
	10:00		3:00		8:00	
	11:00		4:00		9:00	
	12:00		5:00		10:00	

Notes:

Priorities:

Tuesday		Morning		Afternoon		Evening
	8:00		1:00		6:00	
	9:00		2:00		7:00	
	10:00		3:00		8:00	
	11:00		4:00		9:00	
	12:00		5:00		10:00	

Notes:

Priorities:

Wednesday		Morning		Afternoon		Evening
	8:00		1:00		6:00	
	9:00		2:00		7:00	
	10:00		3:00		8:00	
	11:00		4:00		9:00	
	12:00		5:00		10:00	

Notes:

Priorities:

Thursday		Morning		Afternoon		Evening
	8:00		1:00		6:00	
	9:00		2:00		7:00	
	10:00		3:00		8:00	
	11:00		4:00		9:00	
	12:00		5:00		10:00	

Notes:

Priorities:

Friday		Morning		Afternoon		Evening
	8:00		1:00		6:00	
	9:00		2:00		7:00	
	10:00		3:00		8:00	
	11:00		4:00		9:00	
	12:00		5:00		10:00	

Notes:

Priorities:

Weekend		Morning		Afternoon		Evening
	8:00		1:00		6:00	
	9:00		2:00		7:00	
	10:00		3:00		8:00	
	11:00		4:00		9:00	
	12:00		5:00		10:00	

Notes:

Priorities:

Notes

Notes

Notes

Contacts

Name:

Phone:

Address:

Email:

Name:

Phone:

Address:

Email:

Name:

Phone:

Address:

Email:

Name:

Phone:

Address:

Email:

Name:

Phone:

Address:

Email:

Contacts

Name:

Phone:

Address:

Email:

Name:

Phone:

Address:

Email:

Name:

Phone:

Address:

Email:

Name:

Phone:

Address:

Email:

Name:

Phone:

Address:

Email:

To see our complete line of journals, planners, and notebooks visit:

ritchiemedia.ca

Follow Ritchie Media on:

Facebook.com/ritchiemedia

Instagram.com/ritchiemediaptbo

ritchie media, peterborough, on, canada

www.ingramcontent.com/pod-product-compliance
Lightning Source LLC
Chambersburg PA
CBHW082255220526
45469CB00009B/3019